Training Skills
for Supervisors

Training Skills for Supervisors

ROBERT W. LUCAS

Business Skills Express Series

IRWIN
Professional Publishing

MIRROR PRESS

Burr Ridge, Illinois
New York, New York
Boston, Massachusetts

IRWIN
Concerned About Our Environment

In recognition of the fact that our company is a large end-user of fragile yet replenishable resources, we at IRWIN can assure you that every effort is made to meet or exceed Environmental Protection Agency (EPA) recommendations and requirements for a "greener" workplace.

To preserve these natural assets, a number of environmental policies, both companywide and department-specific, have been implemented. From the use of 50% recycled paper in our textbooks to the printing of promotional materials with recycled stock and soy inks to our office paper recycling program, we are committed to reducing waste and replacing environmentally unsafe products with safer alternatives.

Mirror Press:	David R. Helmstadter
	Carla F. Tishler
Editor-in-chief:	Jeffrey A. Krames
Project editor:	Amy E. Lund
Production supervisor:	Diane Palmer
Interior designer:	Laurie Entringer
Cover designer:	Tim Kaage
Art manager:	Kim Meriwether
Art studio:	Electra Graphics, Inc.
Compositor:	Alexander Graphics, Inc.
Typeface:	12/14 Criterion Book
Printer:	Malloy Lithographing, Inc.

Library of Congress Cataloging-in-Publication Data

Lucas, Robert W.
    Training skills for supervisors / Robert W. Lucas.
        p.   cm. — (Business skills express series)
        ISBN 0-7863-0313-1 (alk. paper)
        1. Employees—Training of . 2. Employee training personnel—Training of . 3. Supervisors—Training of . I. Title. II. Series.
    HF5549.5.T7L76   1994
    658.3'124—dc20   94–4999

Printed in the United States of America
1 2 3 4 5 6 7 8 9 0 ML 1 0 9 8 7 6 5 4

PREFACE

More than ever, organizations are being forced to do more with less. To accomplish that, today's employees are being asked to learn new skills, take on additional responsibilities, and continue to help increase bottom line profit without adding additional expense.

To help accomplish these feats, you and other supervisors are being called to fill many roles in the workplace. None of these roles is more crucial than that of trainer. By assuming this key function, you can have significant impact on the organization.

Your job as trainer and coach starts as soon as an employee becomes part of your team. At that point, you must begin to provide guidance and support. You must personally teach or arrange for training that allows your employees to successfully perform their assigned job tasks. Many supervisors shy away from training because they feel unprepared or uncomfortable making group presentations and providing one-on-one coaching. Some believe that training is someone else's job. In fact, training is a prime responsibility for supervisors and does not have to be difficult. It is simply a form of performance coaching.

Training Skills for Supervisors is beneficial for supervisors who are new to training or who want to expand their knowledge of adult learning and training techniques to better transfer knowledge and skills to their employees. Whether making group presentations or coaching one-on-one, this book gives valuable information and insights to make your job as a trainer easier and more effective.

As you explore the contents of this book and later apply the techniques described on the job, you'll become more adept at helping your employees and organization reach company goals and increase productivity. Good luck!

Robert William Lucas

ABOUT THE AUTHOR

Robert William Lucas is the training manager at the national office of the American Automobile Association in Heathrow, Florida. He has extensive experience in the training and development as well as other management fields. For the past 22 years, he has conducted training in a variety of business, government, and volunteer environments. His areas of expertise include management and training program development, interpersonal communication, adult learning, customer service, and employee development.

Mr. Lucas has served on the board of directors for the Metropolitan Chapter of the American Society for Training and Development in Washington, D.C., and in Orlando, Florida, where he is currently president-elect. Additionally, he has given presentations to various local and national groups and serves on a variety of product advisory committees for several national organizations.

Recent publications include two books in this series entitled, *Coaching Skills: A Guide for Supervisors* and *Effective Interpersonal Relationships*. He has also written a leader's guide for the American Management Association video, *Making Your Point without Saying a Word*, training exercises in the *1992 and 1994 Annual: Developing Human Resources* by Pfeiffer & Company; and numerous management and training articles.

Mr. Lucas holds a bachelor of science degree from the University of Maryland and a master of arts degree, with a focus in human resource management, from George Mason University.

ABOUT IRWIN PROFESSIONAL PUBLISHING

Irwin Professional Publishing is the nation's premier publisher of business books. As a Times Mirror company, we work closely with Times Mirror training organizations, including Zenger-Miller, Inc., Learning International, Inc., and Kaset International to serve the training needs of business and industry.

About the Business Skills Express Series

This expanding series of authoritative, concise, and fast-paced books delivers high-quality training on key business topics at a remarkably affordable cost. The series will help managers, supervisors, and frontline personnel in organizations of all sizes and types hone their business skills while enhancing job performance and career satisfaction.

Business Skills Express books are ideal for employee seminars, independent self-study, on-the-job training, and classroom-based instruction. Express books are also convenient-to-use references at work.

CONTENTS

Chapter 8   83

Professional Development

Training Resources 84

Post-Test

89

Self-Assessment

Your ability to develop the knowledge and skills of your employees while shaping their work attitudes depends on many factors. This self-assessment will help you identify focus areas. Using the key below, rate yourself on each statement.

KEY: 1 = Rarely   2 = Sometimes   3 = Frequently   4 = Usually   5 = Always

---

_____ **1.** I identify specific trainee and organizational needs before considering the use of one-on-one or group training activities.

_____ **2.** I consciously attempt to add to my personal network of training contacts.

_____ **3.** I continuously update my knowledge of adult training and learning strategies.

_____ **4.** When planning training, I ensure that the program content ties into employees' jobs.

_____ **5.** I work to develop and hone effective training skills.

_____ **6.** I follow a sequential process when I begin preparing for a new training program.

_____ **7.** As soon as my trainees arrive, I attempt to determine their knowledge, skill, or attitude level in relationship to the program I am going to present.

_____ **8.** I vary my opening remarks and approach based on the training program content and audience.

_____ **9.** I am aware of the impact of training aids and use them appropriately.

_____ **10.** I actively anticipate potential training needs and seek resources to address them.

Scoring:
45–50	Excellent. You have strong training knowledge.
40–44	Very Good. Continue to hone your training knowledge and skills.
30–39	Good. You have a basic knowledge but there is room for improvement.
20–29	Fair. Tap into the resources outlined in Chapter 8 to build your knowledge and skills.
Below 20	Poor. Before attempting to train employees, take the time to gain knowledge and expertise in training skills.

1 | What Is Training?

This chapter will help you to:

- Realize what training *is not*.
- Define the spectrum of training.
- Identify your role in the training process.
- Describe the two categories of training.
- Support the need for training in your organization.

Manny Lopez has just come from a meeting with his supervisor, Twyla Berger. After nearly an hour of discussion, Manny was unsuccessful in convincing Twyla to budget more money to hire a consultant to train Manny's 32 person production staff. Although Manny had clearly explained the training his employees would need to operate the new C412 assembly equipment, Twyla would not concede. She contended that it was *Manny's* job to design and deliver the training. In fact, she wanted him to train all three shifts—more than 100 employees.

At this point, Manny is not only frustrated, but also secretly terrified at the prospect of taking on such an important task. He has never done formal training and is not sure that he can make a presentation in front of a group. ■

1

■ **Q u e s t i o n s   t o   C o n s i d e r**

What do you believe may have prompted Twyla to make her decision?

_____

_____

Is it reasonable to expect a supervisor to take on a task similar to Manny's? Explain.

_____

_____

Do you think Manny's feelings about training are unusual? Explain.

_____

_____

TRAINING IS NOT . . .

An easy way to define training is to tell what it is not. Training is not:

- **A remedy for all performance problems.** The best training in the world cannot change an employee who is incapable of or unwilling to perform a task.

- **A means for an employee to perfect task performance.** In an effective training session, your employees should learn the correct way to perform a task, have their questions answered, and have an opportunity to experiment with their knowledge or skills. They can hone and perfect their techniques on the job when properly supported by you.

- **A way of compensating for poor supervision.** Training is just another tool in your supervisory toolbox. If you do not get actively involved in training or reinforcing the training received by your employees, you both fail.

1

- **Easy.** A successful training session requires forethought and planning. It is not to be taken lightly or done on the spur of the moment as a quick fix for a performance problem. If the latter occurs, you can be sure that the result will be failure—yours and your employees'.

In this book, we define training as: *any formal or informal activity that contributes to an improvement in an employee's knowledge, skill, and attitude levels.*

Training is different from *education,* which conjures up images of school classrooms, concepts, and theories as opposed to the practical application of knowledge. Generally, training is either formal or informal. Some examples of each follow.

Formal	Informal
Classroom presentations.	One-on-one coaching.
Computer-based training.	Peer coaching.
Role-playing.	Correspondence courses.
College courses.	Research.
One-on-one coaching.	

No matter which type of training you do, don't ever hint that your training is insignificant in content or importance. If your employees perceive that you do not support or believe in the training content or method, they will likely follow your lead. Learning, or transfer of knowledge, takes place only when you show commitment, and your employees buy into the effort.

To accomplish this, be prepared to provide informal one-on-one training to your employees as well as formal classroom instruction. Your effectiveness in accomplishing this determines your success rate and that of your employees. You will learn more about one-on-one training in Chapter 5.

Supervisors working with their employees make solid training teams.

Why Train?

There are numerous driving forces behind the need for employee training:

- Change is a constant factor in today's workplace.
- Technology is moving at such a fast pace that many employees and organizations can't keep up.
- Globalization, increased access to world markets, and international competition are growing.
- Supervisors and managers need a broader depth of knowledge to successfully manage a better-educated and more diverse workforce.
- The values and beliefs of today's workforce have changed.
- Demographic shifts in the population of the United States have decreased the pool of qualified entry-level employees; this has led to cross-training (training employees to perform multiple workplace tasks).
- Supervisors are responsible for helping introduce their new employees to company practices and culture; this ensures maximum effectiveness and efficiency on the job.

1

FOSTERING A LEARNING ENVIRONMENT

Each year, all types of organizations feel the impact of social and techno-logical changes. Those organizations that survive and flourish have man-agements that accept and adapt to change. Even though change is often initially rejected and can be painful, it cannot be ignored. Sears, Roebuck and Company; IBM; and several U.S. automakers have made the grave mistake of underestimating the effect of failing to address change. Now they struggle to hold on to what is left and regain their lost market shares. Training is one strategy for reestablishing a foothold.

Support for training in any organization has to start at the top levels of management. If upper managers do not recognize the need for and sup-port training initiatives, your efforts to design and deliver programs will likely fail. The challenge for you and other supervisors is to develop and follow a strategy for employee development that is visible to upper man-agement and that enhances your worth, while adding value to the organi-zation. In the process, you can help your employees evolve to their fullest potential.

BE A CHANGE LEADER

Here are some ways you can develop your strategy and sell your ideas to management:

- **Conduct a training needs assessment.** Outline where you are, where you need to be, resources available, potential barriers, and any other specific areas based on your organizational situation. (There is more information on determining training needs in Chapter 4).

- **Research the field of training and development.** There are hun-dreds of books, articles, and training resources published each year. Read as many varied viewpoints as possible to get a broad perspective on what training can and cannot do for you, your employees, and your organization.

1

- **Partner with others.** Search your organization to identify other supervisors or management members who have training experience and political influence. Meet with them, sell them on your ideas, and either seek their advice or join forces with them to advance your efforts.

- **Network throughout your industry.** Many organizations are providing training to their employees. Rather than start from scratch, contact related organizations and ask them to share resources. If they do not have current training programs or strategies, a potential cost/resource-sharing arrangement might be possible between your organization and theirs.

- **Develop an action plan.** Answer these questions: (1) Who will do what? (2) What needs to be done? (3) When must it occur? (4) How will you proceed? (5) Why are you taking specific action? The latter answer is vital in selling ideas to upper management.

Expanding on What You Have Learned

Take a few minutes to think about the concepts and information covered in this chapter. Build on your knowledge by answering the following questions.

1. What are some key benefits of effective training?

   _____

   _____

2. How can you dispel some of the common misperceptions about the purpose of training?

   _____

   _____

3. If you were attempting to convince someone else in your workplace of the importance of training, what would say?

   _____

   _____

4. What training knowledge do you need to provide or support employee training in your organization?

_____

_____

1

Chapter 1 Checkpoints

Training your employees is an important supervisory role. To fulfill that role effectively, you must continue to develop not only a positive attitude about training and development but also the skills to provide or support training initiatives. Keep the following points in mind:

✓ Training is an *additional* tool, not an answer to all performance problems.

✓ It is your responsibility to introduce new employees to your company culture.

✓ Training is any formal or informal activity that contributes to an improvement in an employee's knowledge, skills, and attitude.

✓ You must develop and follow a solid strategy to help effect training in your organization.

2 | Understanding How Adults Learn

This chapter will help you to: ─────────

- Recognize key differences between the way children and adults learn.
- Identify specific principles of adult learning.
- Determine participant learning styles.
- Develop strategies for training employees effectively.

Helen Marshal is reviewing the evaluation forms from a customer service program she conducted for her employees today. Helen is confused and a bit upset by the results. On a scale of 1 (Poor) to 7 (Outstanding), she received numerous ratings of 1 to 4 in the areas of "Training environment," "Presenter effectiveness," "Relevance to the job," and "Ability to involve participants."

Helen can't figure out what went wrong. She made sure that participants had all the materials they needed and the room was organized before they arrived. She even made sure that the rows of chairs were perfectly aligned to present a good first impression. As she gave her lecture, she periodically asked if there were questions, but got little response. She also provided a nice set of handouts at the end of the presentation so the trainees would have reference material. ■

2

■ **Q u e s t i o n s t o C o n s i d e r**

Considering Helen's program topic and the manner in which she presented the information, could she have neglected trainees' expectations? Explain.

_____

_____

Could Helen have done anything differently to change the outcome? Explain.

_____

_____

Many supervisors train ineffectively. This is often caused by their lack of training knowledge or experience. Since they likely have little foundation in formal adult learning techniques, they draw from their own previous learning experiences in religious training, schools, colleges, or professional lectures. While those methods were useful and effective in their original settings, they may not be in an employee training environment.

ADULT VERSUS CHILD LEARNING

Researchers have studied the differences in the ways people learn since the late 1920s. Although adults and children share some similarities, they differ in learning preferences, needs, and responses to various elements of the training process.

Traditionally, educators assumed that children were like blank slates waiting to be filled with knowledge or information. Therefore, all learning decisions were generally made for children by their teachers. On the other hand, adults have distinctly different needs and perceptions about how training should be conducted. Some of the key differences between adult and child learners follow:

▪ **Adults want to know the benefit of what they learn.** They often ask and need to be told what the _Added Value And Results For Me_

(AVARFM) is before buying into the concepts or ideas presented. They need to see how the training ties into real-world issues. On the other hand, children may accept "someday you'll need this" as a reason to listen.

- **Adults expect to participate in learning.** Often, they can tie previous knowledge and experience into program content and relate it to what they already know. This expedites and enhances learning. Since children have limited life experience, they depend more heavily on their teachers' guidance and knowledge.

- **Adults are motivated by intrinsic needs or desires.** Generally, adult learners attend training programs because they want or need the content information to do their jobs or improve personally. Children attend because they are directed by others.

- **Adult learning is usually competency based.** Generally, training programs help adults perform better on the job. Child learning tends to be short-term, with an immediate goal, focused on passing a test.

- **Adult training environments are varied.** Depending on the program, content, activities planned, and instructor, the room configuration often varies. Child training environments tend to be rows of desks facing a teacher who lectures with little variety.

ADULT LEARNING PRINCIPLES

As you can see, there are numerous differences between adult and child learners. From these differences you can derive basic principles concerning adult training to develop and deliver more effective programs for your employees. Some key principles follow:

- **Relate training to the job.** Show how employees can immediately apply what they learn in the workplace. Identify this relationship in opening remarks and program objectives.

- **Make the training experience FUN!** Don't prohibit people from enjoying their learning experience. Be creative. Use props, prizes,

2

decorations, techniques, activities, or anything that stimulates learning and retention.

- **Involve participants.** Use your trainees as resources by soliciting volunteers to help facilitate activities, share knowledge, or demonstrate concepts or techniques.

- **Remain flexible and adaptable.** If you determine during training that there are other needs related to your topic or that your planned material or activities are not working, be willing to change.

- **Create a motivating and functional learning environment.** Plan and organize your learning environment to support and facilitate training. Make sure you have arranged tables and materials effectively before participants arrive.

- **Treat trainees as adults.** Acknowledge their levels of expertise, tap into the group's knowledge, and do not talk down to participants.

▪ **Recognize learner knowledge and experience.** Build program content around the level of knowledge or experience your trainees already possess. Reinventing or reviewing what they already know wastes valuable time and bores participants.

2

■ **P e r s o n a l   R e f l e c t i o n**

Take a few minutes to think about one training program you have attended or presented that ignored one or more of the adult learning principles just outlined.

Which principles were ignored?

_____

_____

What was the result of the omission?

_____

_____

Specifically, what could have been done to address the principles omitted and improve the program?

_____

_____

LEARNING STYLE PREFERENCE

In addition to understanding the basic principles that influence adult learning, you should be conscious that trainees gain knowledge in different ways. These preferences are *learning styles*.

People get and process information by using three learning styles. They may prefer one, two, all three, or a combination of the three in gathering information. The three styles involve visual, aural, and kinesthetic learning.

Visual Learners

Visual learners get the most understanding and learning when they see or mentally visualize information, processes, or concepts. Sometimes they use language such as:

- I have a good picture of what you're saying.
- It appears to me . . .
- I believe I can see what you mean.
- I see your point.
- As I see it, the situation is . . .

To appeal to and address the needs of visual learners, include some of the following in your program:

- Videos.
- 35mm slides.
- Transparencies
- Posters.
- Handouts.
- Graphs.
- Photos.
- Actual items.
- Charts.
- Demonstrations.

Aural Learners

Aural learners gather information and comprehend key points through listening. They sometimes use language such as:

- If I'm hearing you correctly . . .
- It sounds like you are saying . . .
- What you're saying is music to my ears.
- As I hear it, the situation is . . .
- I hear exactly what you are saying.

To appeal to and address the needs of aural learners, use some of the following in your programs:

- Videos.
- Audiocassettes.
- Group discussions.
- Instructor-led dialogue.

- Music.
- Interactive videos.
- Panel discussions.
- Debates.

Kinestheic Learners

Kinesthetic learners gather information and gain maximum understanding by performing a task or being personally involved in the learning activity. They sometimes say things like:

- I've got a firm grip on what you're saying.
- It feels to me as if . . .
- I can't quite grasp what you mean . . .
- Let's pick the problem apart and see what we've got.
- Let's jump in and get started.

To address the needs of kinesthetic learners, use some of the following techniques:

- Roleplaying.
- Demonstrations.
- Practical application.
- Tests.
- Actual items (equipment or tools they actually use on the job).
- In-basket exercises. (Skill-building and evaluation activities in which trainees must sort through a variety of forms, correspondence, or documents resembling those they use in their jobs. Based on what

they are given, they must make decisions on courses of action, distribution, etc.)

- Games.
- Interactive videos.
- Field trips.
- Simulations.

From a training perspective, if you know your trainees' learning styles, you can design programs and materials to target those styles. Additionally, by recognizing your own preferences, you can avoid designing materials and activities from your preference perspective. Remember that not everyone learns in the same manner you do. For example, if you prefer to learn visually, you may unconsciously use a lot of transparencies, slides, or flipcharts; these choices ignore the other two learning styles.

To determine your own learning style, complete the following survey. Before conducting a training session, distribute this survey form to your trainees, so you can consider their learning styles as you prepare your materials.

PREFERRED LEARNING STYLE SURVEY

To determine your preferred learning styles, read each question, then place an X in the column of the statement that applies to you in a training environment.

TD = Totally Disagree   D = Disagree   N = Neutral   A = Agree   TA = Totally Agree

	TD	D	N	A	TA
1. I learn best by performing a task or activity.	___	___	___	___	___
2. I like to read descriptions and use pictures, drawings, and diagrams when I learn.	___	___	___	___	___
3. I prefer to read material rather than listen to tapes.	___	___	___	___	___
4. I'd rather attempt a task without reading about or having it explained to me.	___	___	___	___	___
5. I learn best by practicing on the job.	___	___	___	___	___
6. I need to see something to remember it.	___	___	___	___	___
7. I prefer to hear about how something is done.	___	___	___	___	___
8. I retain more when someone describes something to me.	___	___	___	___	___
9. I find it hard to master a task I have not practiced.	___	___	___	___	___
10. I enjoy programs In which groups have time to discuss issues.	___	___	___	___	___
11. I have difficulty recalling information when training aids and handouts are omitted.	___	___	___	___	___
12. I prefer listening to tapes rather than reading about a topic.	___	___	___	___	___

Scoring Key: Questions 2, 3, 6, 11 indicate visual learning preference.

Questions 7, 8, 10, 12 indicate aural learning preference.

Questions 1, 4, 5, 9, indicate kinesthetic learning preference.

Note: You may have multiple preferences.

■ Expanding on What You Have Learned

Now that you have had a chance to identify and think about some of the specific differences in the way people learn, take a few minutes to answer these questions.

1. Are there currently programs in your organization that ignore the principles identified in this chapter? If yes, identify them.

   _____

   _____

2. What opportunities exist to incorporate principles concerning adult learning into your current or planned training programs?

   _____

   _____

3. Is there anyone with adult learning or training experience you can recruit to help with training?

   _____

   _____

Chapter 2 Checkpoints

As you evaluate and/or develop your training programs, keep the following points in mind;

✓ In many cases, adult learning needs differ significantly from those of children.

✓ For adults to get maximum benefit from training, they must buy into what is being presented. When they can answer the question, What is the Added Value And Results For Me?, adults participate and learn.

✓ Teach adults real-life, competency-based skills and encourage participation in the training.

✓ Learning environments and activities should support and enhance learning.

✓ Know your own learning preferences and those of your trainees when designing and delivering training.

3 | Developing Training Skills

This chapter will help you to:

- Explain why supervisors often make good trainers.
- Identify the characteristics of an effective trainer.
- Recognize the areas of skill development needed to be a successful trainer.

Joel Peters, auto claims supervisor for Westlake Insurance Company, learned this morning that he has been assigned to the corporate training staff for 12 months. Even though Joel has only been with the company for a little over a year, he is one of seven people identified as superstars and placed on the fast track for advancement. Key among his skills is the ability to make sound decisions and interact with a variety of people.

Under Westlake's new loaned manager program, designed to cross-train selected supervisors and managers over the next five years, Joel will begin on-the-job training in four weeks with the training and development department. While pleased by the opportunity, Joel is a bit apprehensive since he has not conducted formal training before.

To help prepare for the new position, Joel has arranged to meet the training manager tomorrow to discuss expectations and duties. Joel knows that initially he will be responsible for providing subject matter expertise for revisions of current insurance

3

sales programs and those in development. He will also co-facilitate future programs for a variety of corporate personnel. ■

■ Q u e s t i o n s   t o   C o n s i d e r

What value can Joel bring to his new assignment?

_____

_____

How can Joel apply his strengths in his new position?

_____

_____

In addition to meeting with the training manager, what steps might Joel take to prepare for his assignment?

_____

_____

Based on your experience and what was discussed in previous chapters, what skills must Joel master in his new job?

_____

_____

Supervisors as Trainers

Supervisors often make good trainers for a variety of reasons; they:

- Have a vested interest in ensuring employees are adequately trained. If the employee fails on the job, so does the supervisor.
- Have already established rapport with employees.
- Are credible and knowledgeable of required procedures and on-the-job challenges.
- Know how to relate classroom information to the job environment.

- Speak the same jargon as their employees.
- Know what was taught in the classroom and can continue to reinforce the learning on the job.

CHARACTERISTICS OF AN EFFECTIVE TRAINER

While planning to assume formal and informal training roles, you must examine those characteristics that separate excellent from average trainers. To be a successful trainer, you should possess many of the following attributes:

- **A willingness to learn.** You can enhance your own knowledge and skills levels while facilitating the learning of others. Every time you prepare a presentation or encounter an individual or group in a training environment, try to absorb and assimilate information. Your employees probably have a lot of good ideas, experience, and past knowledge that can benefit your professional growth. Also, by demonstrating that you are open to their input, you can develop and enhance communication with your employees.

- **Solid leadership ability.** Your trainees look to you for guidance and direction. To fulfill your role as trainer you need to be organized, focused, and able to set an example without being autocratic. Keep in mind that adult learners don't like being lectured to or being told everything. They want to participate.

- **Consulting and mentoring skills.** Training does not end once your employee leaves the classroom or completes a learning assignment. You need to follow up, evaluate progress, and provide ongoing guidance and updates. The end of formal training marks the beginning of your coaching phase. Through continued observation and follow-up, you can facilitate transfer of knowledge from the classroom to the workplace.

- **Motivational skills.** Attaining new levels of knowledge or skill and changing attitudes can be difficult for some employees. They need your continued support before, during, and after training to succeed. Some-times, simply knowing that you trust and believe in them helps employ-ees master new material. To accomplish your role as motivator, you must not only understand what motivates your employees but also help address their needs. Because motivation comes from within, create a learning and supporting environment that develops self-motivation.

■ **Knowledge of subjects taught.** It is vital that you have a sound understanding of the subject matter. Adult learners are very good at rec-ognizing incompetence or lack of expertise. If you do not know your sub-ject, your credibility drops.

This does not mean you must know every detail about a task or sub-ject. You should have a solid foundation, however, and know where to get answers to questions you cannot address.

■ **Sincere desire to train.** Employees who suspect that your heart is not in your efforts are likely to lack enthusiasm. To be most effective, you need to show zest in teaching them. If you view the training as drudgery, examine the reason and ask yourself what you can do to rekindle the spark. When you cannot overcome your dislike, get someone else to train the employees; otherwise, you are doing the employees, yourself, and the organization a disservice.

■ **Patience.** Not all trainees have the same abilities or learn at the same rate. Be sure to pace your training so that all trainees benefit. If one person seems to be having difficulty mastering information or tech-niques, find out why. If the person has a learning disability and you fail to address this, you could be violating the Americans with Disabilities Act of 1990 by not providing equal access to training. You may have to modify the training, do individual tutoring, or assign a peer coach.

■ **Flexibility.** In training others, you can expect things to go wrong. People, facilities, or equipment may not be available when planned, equipment may malfunction, someone may interrupt training, or any number of things may go contrary to your plan. Additionally, you may find that scheduled activities or techniques may be ineffective in addressing your trainees' needs. To compensate for this possibility, plan alternatives.

Personal Reflection

Think of a past supervisor or manager who successfully trained you.

What made the person most effective as a trainer?

____

____

What would have made her even more effective?

____

____

Of the characteristics that contributed to the person's effectiveness, which do you possess?

____

____

DEVELOP FACILITATION SKILLS

In addition to possessing the characteristics of an effective trainer you need to develop or hone your skills in the following areas to have meaningful training programs:

Presentation Skills

Five sub-skills are important:

1. Listening. To be effective as a trainer, you must be a good listener. You have to depend on aurally gathering information as you prepare or design your programs, deliver the training, and get feedback during training and evaluation.

2. Oral communication. Oral communication includes effective use of your voice (rate, volume, inflection, tone), vocabulary, and the ability to formulate and deliver messages that audience members can understand. Much of your success rests on your ability to communicate your knowledge and ideas during training. For that reason, solid oral communication skills are vital.

3. Nonverbal communication skills. In concert with your verbal delivery, nonverbal cues are crucial. You must understand what nonverbal cues potentially mean, how to use them, and how to interpret the cues your trainees send. During your presentation or interactions with trainees, you deliver much of your message through your body language (dress, gestures, eye contact, and movement). Before attempting to train, rehearse your presentation while videotaping yourself. As you review the tape later, honestly critique what you see and make necessary changes. (For additional information on nonverbal communication, see another of my books in this series, *Effective Interpersonal Relationships.*

4. Questioning. To encourage participants' involvement, determine their understanding of points made, and get feedback, you must be adept at phrasing and asking questions. Think about and practice your questioning technique to fine tune your ability to ask questions and respond effectively to those asked of you. Some basic tips for asking questions follow:

- Ask questions often. Asking questions provides an opportunity for trainee involvement and for you to verify understanding. It also increases the flow of two-way communication, making the training more interactive.

- Avoid leading questions. Questions that begin with "Don't you think?" or "Wouldn't you agree?" neither encourage thinking nor solicit real trainee input.

- Do not embarrass trainees. Using questions designed to pigeonhole or punish trainees can backfire and cause their peers to side with them against you. Embarrassing questions also create barriers to learning. Asking a direct question to someone who obviously does not know an answer or is caught daydreaming, does little to advance your cause.

3

Common Body Language Signals

Personal appearance. The way you dress and your accessories and grooming send distinct messages based on the receiver's perspective.

Gestures. The manner in which you use or fail to use your hands sends messages. For example, standing with your hands in your pockets or behind you could indicate nervousness or uncertainty about what to do with them. Pointing a finger could be threatening or rude. Overuse of gestures or extreme animation could be distracting.

Eye contact. It is said that the eyes are the windows to the soul. You can send a message of openness and friendship, of trying to hide something, or of being insecure; it all depends on how well you establish eye contact. A general rule of thumb in a training environment is to make eye contact (generally no more than 5 to 10 seconds) with every trainee at some point during your program.

Movement. You can emphasize key points, potentially intimidate, or solicit involvement by participants simply by your movements. For example, if two participants were talking and distracting others, you could move, stand next to them, and make eye contact. Nonverbally you would be saying "Shut up."

- Use open-ended questions. Asking yes/no (or closed) questions does not expand the material presented and actually limits dialogue. For example, instead of asking, "Michelle, is this how you would handle the task?" ask, "Michelle, how would you handle the task?"

- Don't be a know-it-all. Turn questions asked of you back to the group for response. For example, after receiving a question, turn to other participants and ask, "What do the rest of you think about . . . ?" or "What advice can the rest of you give about . . . ?" Another option is to return the question to the person who initiated it by responding, "Interesting question, Rick. What do you see as a possible solution?"

3

- Call on different trainees. Do not allow one person to monopolize the conversation. When one person continues to volunteer, acknowledge that trainee and state, "Let's give some others a chance to express their thoughts."

- Vary questioning techniques. By asking questions in different ways, you add variety while helping to maintain interest. Two possibilities are the APC or CPA techniques.

  1. **A**sk the question of no one in particular. This alerts everyone and gets them thinking of possible responses.
     Pause in order for trainees to think about the question.
     Call on one person for a response.
  2. **C**all on a specific person. This gets his attention and involvement.
     Pause to allow trainees to focus their attention and listen.
     Ask the question.

- Avoid stacking questions. Do not ask a second question before you get a response to the first one. For example, "Sandy, what do you think the potential is for . . . ?" "Do you believe other problems could arise as a result of . . . ?" In this example, the confused trainee may not know which question to answer first or may get off the subject in responding to the second question and forget the first.

- Allow time to respond. It is very frustrating for a trainer to ask a question of one trainee and then before a response can be given, call on someone else. Remember that a trainee's silence does not necessarily mean ignorance, it can indicate that the person is analyzing the question and formulating a response.

- Avoid trick questions. Adults do not appreciate being made to look foolish, especially in front of their peers. Asking questions to which you know there is no real answer or which embarrass the trainee causes resentment and may block future communication. You may create a barrier between yourself and all trainees. People won't respond to questions that simply allow you and others an opportunity to laugh at them.

Chapter 6 contains additional information on questioning.

5. Feedback. You need to give feedback during all phases of training development and delivery. To provide feedback effectively, try the six-step process in Chapter 5.

Writing Skills

Simply having subject knowledge is not enough. Your training role requires that you capture ideas in a clear, concise, and logical manner to produce lesson outlines, handouts, and training materials.

Interpersonal Relations Skills

Since you deal with a variety of employees during training, you must effectively forge and develop relationships. These relationships are based on trust and smooth interaction. Another book in this series, *Effective Interpersonal Relationships*, provides suggestions for improvement in this area.

Decision-Making Skills

Throughout the entire cycle of assessing needs and designing, developing, delivering, and evaluating your training programs, you must make sound, timely, and efficient decisions. The way you deal with challenges and questions reflects on your ability to effectively do your job.

Group Facilitation Skills

Dividing trainees into small groups, instructing, facilitating, and then debriefing them following activities seems easy. It often isn't, especially for the new trainer. Small group facilitation requires forethought and practice to make it appear effortless and to produce the desired results. Numerous books deal with group facilitation.

3

■ Personal Reflection

Which of the skills or attributes listed in this chapter do you currently have, and which need further development? Make a list here for future reference.

_____

_____

■ Expanding on What You Have Learned

With the knowledge of why supervisors potentially make good trainers and the characteristics and skills of effective instructors fresh in your mind, answer the following questions:

1. How can an awareness of the characteristics and skill sets required for trainers aid in your personal development? Explain.

   _____

   _____

2. What special talents, knowledge, and skills do you currently have that will aid in your performance as a trainer?

   _____

   _____

3. In your training role, which areas of personal development need more work?

   _____

   _____

4. What specific resources can you tap to develop your training knowledge or skills?

   _____

   _____

Chapter 3 Checkpoints

As you prepare an action plan for developing your training skills, keep the following in mind:

✓ As a supervisor, you currently possess numerous attributes that can ensure your success as a trainer.

✓ To be effective in facilitating training, you need to be willing to learn.

✓ A sincere desire to train others is important, as are patience, flexibility, and a knowledge of subjects you teach.

✓ To be effective, you need to have good presentation, writing, interpersonal relations, decision-making, and group facilitation skills.

4 | The Training Process Model

This chapter will help you to:

- Recognize the steps in a formal training process.
- Identify how to prepare to train your employees as a group.
- Develop a strategy for planning your next training program.
- Justify materials, staff, equipment, and facilities for your next training session.

When Jack Lewis, corporate training manager of Your Way Supermarkets, picked up the phone he heard, "Help!" On the other end of the line was Linda Rondale, produce supervisor for the Hamilton branch store. She told Jack her manager just asked her to conduct an employee safety training program for the entire day shift. Linda said, "I haven't a clue where to begin, Jack. Sure, I've attended some sessions your people have taught, but I don't know anything about training."

Jack interrupted, "Slow down, Linda. It'll be all right. You just need to do a little preparation." He continued, "Let's meet and discuss this further. How does 4:00 PM on Thursday sound?" "Great" exclaimed Linda. "I need all the help I can get. Thanks." ■

▮ Questions to Consider

Does this scenario sound unusual? Explain.

_____

_____

What would you do if you were in Linda's place?

_____

_____

List some steps Linda would have to take to get ready for her class.

_____

_____

As is often the case, a key role of a supervisor is that of trainer. For that reason, you may find yourself facing a dilemma similar to Linda's. And, if you are like many other supervisors, you can use some guidelines for preparing and conducting training.

WHAT IS THE TRAINING PROCESS MODEL?

Numerous process models can help you design a formal training program. Like the Training Process Model (TPM), most are based on the *Instructional Systems Design (ISD)* process used by the U.S. military since World War II. The TPM provides specific steps to follow in developing and delivering training. Whether you have a company training staff or not, you may want to develop your own programs and materials. TPM includes five distinct phases that prepare you to take on the role of trainer.

PHASE ONE—IDENTIFY NEEDS

Training needs can develop rapidly or over a period of time in the workplace. Generally these needs are either personal or organizational.

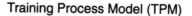

Training Process Model (TPM)

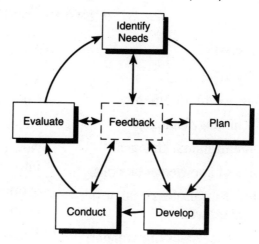

■ **Personal needs result from your employees' lack of knowledge, skills, or attitudes.** These deficits cause an inability to meet established standards or goals; ultimately they could contribute to a breakdown in organizational efficiency. For example, if employees assigned a new task have received no previous training, they would have a need to learn specific information or processes to successfully perform their jobs.

In addition to job-related deficits, employees may desire to advance or change jobs, but lack needed knowledge or skills. This personal need is different; although not required for job success, employees personally need the knowledge to improve their skills.

■ **Organizational needs occur when groups of employees cannot or will not perform within required parameters.** When this happens there is usually a systematic breakdown that, if not adequately addressed in a timely manner, can cause serious production, quality, or service problems.

Assuming you and management believe there is a deficit in performance, you must conduct a needs analysis (sometimes called an *assessment*) as indicated in Chapter 1. This helps determine the type and level of

4

Origins of Needs

Personal

- New to job.
- New job requirements.
- Technology changes.
- Organizational changes.
- Lack of knowledge or skills.
- Desire for professional or personal growth.
- New supervisor or manager.
- Workforce makeup or structure changes.
- Special projects assigned.
- Performance level shifts.

Organizational

- Technology changes.
- Customer or market trend shift.
- Hierarchy or structure changes.
- New products or services introduced.
- Workforce demographic changes.
- Legislation.
- Policy or procedure changes.
- Team or quality initiatives.
- Employee performance changes.
- Turnover trends change.

---

need present in your organization. As a result of doing this analysis, you should be able to answer the following questions:

- What is the need?
- What are indicators of the need?
- What is causing the need?
- Is it an organizationwide, individual, or small group need?
- What are some information sources about the need? (Have there been complaints from customers, peers, or other employees? Can they accurately perform job tasks? Are they meeting production and service standards according to job-related statistics?)
- Is it a system (technology) or a people issue?

- Is management aware of and addressing the issue?
- Is the need internally or externally driven?
- Have previous initiatives addressed this need? If so, what were the results?

By asking these questions, you might determine that training really is not needed. This would mean the problem is due to a system (policy, procedure, or technology) or management breakdown that should be addressed in other ways.

Once you determine the problem is related to employees' knowledge, skills, or attitude deficits, you must consider training. The following questions can help you sharpen your focus:

- Who will make up the target audience?
- What are current knowledge, skill, and attitude levels?
- Which resources (money, people, equipment, facilities, materials, training programs) are available?
- What special needs do trainees have?
- Which factors inside and outside the organization impact training (time, management, resources, instructor knowledge or ability, target population)?

To answer these questions, consider getting information from the following sources:

- Targeted trainees.
- Performance appraisal forms.
- Other supervisors or managers.
- Other trainees.
- Co-workers.
- Interviews (trainees, co-workers, bosses).
- Vendors.

- Exit inteviews.
- Grievance or complaint files.
- Questionnaires.
- Customers.
- Past incumbents in the trainee's job.

PHASE TWO—PLAN

As with all successful ventures, designing a training program requires substantial planning. During the planning phase, continue gathering data and formulate approaches to address the needs you identified in phase one. Some of the decisions during the second phase involve:

Learning Objectives

What knowledge, skills, or attitudes will trainees have at the end of the program? Write these from the standpoint of what the trainee is expected to know or do as a result of the training. According to training experts, learning objectives should contain an action verb and measurable criteria. Write objectives in terms of behavior that can be observed or evaluated; avoid vague terminology that cannot. For example, avoid phrases such as, "The trainee will know" or "The employee will understand." Neither of these can be measured.

Sample Learning Objectives

At the end of this session, trainees will be able to:

- Define the five phases of the training process model.
- Identify questions used to gather information during a training needs analysis.
- Describe two types of training needs.

Program Prerequisites for Learners.

What do learners need to do or accomplish prior to the program? Often learning is based on prior knowledge and skills or begins by having trainees accomplish tasks or assignments prior to the scheduled training date. This advance work might be gathering information for classroom discussion, completing a survey, or taking a pretest to determine knowledge levels.

■ **Length of the program.** Operational commitments (production deadlines, staff assignments, delivery schedules, budget constraints) often dictate time frames for training. How much time is required and can be allocated to address the issue?

4

■ **Training strategies or methodologies.** How can information be delivered? Here are some potential training methods:

- Job rotation.
- Lecture.
- Panel.
- Programmed instruction.
- Games.
- Role-playing.
- Small group discussion.
- Instrumentation (assessments).
- Audiovisual assisted.
- Computer assisted.
- Forum.
- Test.

- Symposium.
- On-the-job coaching.
- Self-study.
- Case study.
- In-basket exercises.
- Simulations.
- Brainstorming.
- Dyad or triad. (Small group activity involving either two or three people.)
- Demonstration.
- Debate.
- Field trip.

■ **Training aids needed.** Which learner or instructor materials, equipment, and supplies can you use? Based on availability of funds, training location, and other resources or factors, the aids and materials you can access may be limited.

Costs

What will you need to purchase, rent, or develop? This factor often has a dramatic impact on the form, type, and duration of your program. If costs seem prohibitive and internal resources are not available, investigate some of the recommendations in Chapter 8.

Audience Size/Population

Who should attend the program? The number of trainees governs your requirement for facilities, equipment, materials, instructors, and the number of times you offer the session.

Instructors Required and Their Qualifications

Are instructors currently on staff or will they have to be recruited? If you or other staff members will conduct the training, consider time constraints and other commitments. If outside resources are used, consider actual requirements and costs.

Testing Strategy

What will be tested? What test format will be used? Testing determines the success of your program and the need for additional training.

Evaluation Method

How will program effectiveness be judged? Consider the techniques in phase five to ensure that your program is as successful and beneficial as possible.

PHASE THREE—DEVELOP

Next to actually conducting the program, you spend most of your time in the development cycle. Development involves preparing a lesson plan or trainer's guide, learners guide, training aids, support materials, tests, and evaluations. Additionally, during this phase you must handle these logistical requirements:

- Ordering and reserving equipment and facilities.
- Ordering print materials (handouts, learner's/leader's guides).
- Procuring training aids (flipcharts, posters, transparencies, slides, videos).
- Coordinating with other instructors and assistants.
- Promoting and announcing the program.
- Registering and coordinating participants.
- Reviewing and modifying existing materials.

Because of the length and complexity of this phase, you can benefit greatly by developing a project plan or using a detailed checklist to prioritize and track task completion. Use the sample training program checklist on page 42 as a model.

PHASE FOUR—CONDUCT

Once you have organized all the details of the program, created the materials you'll need, and rehearsed until you are proficient, you're ready to present your program to an audience. If time permits, do an initial run-through of the program with a select group of participants who have needs and qualifications similar to those of your target audience. Following this

4

SAMPLE TRAINING PROGRAM CHECKLIST

Pretraining	Date To Start	Date To Be Completed
▪ Schedule trainers.	_____	_____
▪ Reserve facility.	_____	_____
▪ Reserve equipment.	_____	_____
▪ Order print materials.	_____	_____
▪ Pick up handouts.	_____	_____
▪ Develop/order training aids.	_____	_____
▪ Pick up training aids.	_____	_____
▪ Consolidate all training materials.	_____	_____
▪ Distribute program announcements		
—Bulletin boards.	_____	_____
—In-house mailing.	_____	_____
▪ Confirm registrants (memo).	_____	_____
Post-training		
▪ Compile evaluation report	_____	_____
▪ Organize leftover materials	_____	_____
▪ Bill attendees	_____	_____
▪ Make necessary revisions to materials	_____	_____
▪ File copy of class roster/evaluations	_____	_____
90 Days Following Training		
▪ Send post-session evaluation to attendees	_____	_____
▪ Collect evaluations/compile results	_____	_____

pilot session, solicit feedback, and modify the program as necessary before offering it to your target population.

PHASE FIVE—EVALUATE

The final phase of TPM involves evaluating your program's format, content, materials, instructors, and logistics. To be most effective, evaluate your program from different perspectives, using one or more of the following processes:

- End of program evaluations, often called *smile sheets,* allow participants to give feedback as soon as the session ends. These forms generally use a rating scale (1 [Poor] to 7 or 10 [Outstanding]) and ask trainees to rate areas such as program content, instructor ability, training aids, and facility. They often ask for overall comments on the program.

If your program extends over several days, use interim evaluations in the form of quizzes, daily evaluations, question and answer sessions, or personal feedback. This allows you to correct problems during the program rather than waiting until the end when implemented changes cannot benefit the current trainees.

- Instructor evaluation involves critically assuring the effectiveness of the leader's guide, support materials, logistics, and training methodologies by you or other instructors. In this form of evaluation, look to see that activities, training aids, and materials address needs discovered through your needs analysis.

- Independent evaluation conducted by a peer or training professional who can give candid feedback and make recommendations for improvement. If you are relatively new to training, seek this type of assistance.

- On-the-job evaluation made by you or other supervisors through direct observation of employees once they return from training. Your goal is to determine if the training has effected changes in knowledge, skills, or attitude. This observation is ongoing but can be formally conducted at increments of one, three, and six months through a formal post-training survey.

Based on the results of the evaluations of your pilot program, return to whichever phase of TPM that seems appropriate. Repeat that phase and subsequent phases in an effort to correct program deficiencies.

4

Feedback in relation to TPM is not as detailed as the feedback referred to in Chapters 3 and 5. TPM feedback refers to the need to verify steps of the process in each phase of the model to prevent oversights.

Although not a formal phase in the model, feedback is crucial in the success of all TPM phases. If candid feedback is not volunteered at each phase, actively solicit it from subject matter experts or other appropriate sources. Without honest input or constructive criticism, you may overlook gaps in the program and fail to meet stated objectives or learner needs.

Expanding on What You Have Learned

With the training process model in mind, take a few minutes to answer the following questions:

1. Do you have employees in your department with personal training needs that should be addressed? What knowledge, skill, or attitudes could be improved by training?

   _____

   _____

2. Which shifts within your organization will need to be addressed by training in your department?

   _____

   _____

3. Based on issues raised in phase two of TPM, which factors does your organization traditionally consider when planning training? Which do you need to address in future programs?

   _____

   _____

4. Of the issues identified in phase three, which do you consider most difficult to deal with? Why?

_____

_____

5. Who else in your department can you call upon to assist in training?

_____

_____

4

Chapter 4 Checkpoints

Before taking any training initiative, remember the following points:

✓ Training needs are either personal or organizational.

✓ To determine needs, consult a variety of sources.

✓ Before spending time, effort, and money on training, ensure the problem is not being caused by a system, policy, technology, or management breakdown.

✓ Take time to adequately plan programs and consider a variety of methodologies to address identified needs.

✓ Use a project plan with timelines when developing programs to ensure you do not overlook anything.

✓ Always try to give a pilot program to get feedback prior to presenting the actual program.

✓ Following the conclusion of training, get immediate feedback and continue to solicit additional information at specified intervals.

✓ Feedback is a crucial part of all phases of TPM.

5 | One-on-One Training

This chapter will help you to:

- Explain how to prepare, conduct, and follow up one-on-one training.
- Develop strategies for conducting one-on-one training.
- Identify successful training techniques.

"I just don't understand. Why can't Tony learn our new procedure for packaging engine parts," complained Frank Watson, supervisor on the third shift at AutoTech Manufacturing. He continued, "I've explained the process over and over. I've talked and talked until I'm blue in the face. Tony still doesn't get it! What's his problem?"

Lori Hamilton, second shift supervisor, said, "Did you try demonstrating? You know, having Tony perform the process, then giving him feedback?" Frank replied, "I didn't think all that was necessary, it's so simple. Tony's a smart guy and keeps telling me he understands. But, he just can't get it right." ∎

■ Questions to Consider

Based on what you learned in Chapter 2, is there anything Frank is overlooking?

_____

_____

What is Lori attempting to do in this scenario?

_____

_____

Do you think Lori was successful? Explain.

_____

_____

What other approaches might Frank use to help Tony master the process?

_____

_____

5

WHAT IS ONE-ON-ONE TRAINING?

Training employees as individuals falls into both the formal and informal categories discussed in Chapter 1. It is another form of performance coaching. There are numerous instances when one-on-one training is more appropriate than a formal group presentation. Some opportunities arise when:

- New employees join your organization and need orientation.
- Changes occur in individual job requirements.
- New equipment arrives or modifications to existing equipment occur.
- Employees experience performance difficulties and require remedial training.
- Preparation for an upcoming special project is needed.

Are there other opportunities for one-on-one training in your company?

STAGES OF TRAINING

Preparing the Session

As with any other process, advance preparation before starting employee training is the key to success. Some basic planning steps include:

1. **Identify the task.** Take a good look at what needs to be accomplished and decide why, how, when, and where training must be done.

2. **Visualize your role.** What will you need to do or facilitate to address knowledge, skill, and attitude issues?

3. **Define the trainee population.** Who needs training?

4. **Plan resources.** Determine which materials, equipment, staff assistance, and facilities you need.

5. **Schedule training.** Ensure that you notify trainees, assistants, logistical and facility coordinators, and anyone else involved.

6. **Prepare a timeline.** Use a timeline as a guide in ordering materials and supplies, reserving training sites outside the workplace, making notifications, and distributing items.

7. **Develop a checklist.** Incorporate items from the timeline along with all the last minute details.

Preparing the Trainees

Once you have planned and prepared to conduct the training, sit down with employees to prepare them for the learning experience.

▪ **Personalize the event.** By establishing rapport through one-to-one dialogue with the trainees you increase chances of successfully communicating ideas and information during the program. Self-disclosure of personal experiences related to the training program and content often helps. For example, if you are conducting personal computer training, you may reduce trainees' anxiety by telling about your own fears, apprehension, and frustration when learning to use the hardware or software. Your disclosure may allay trainees' fears while making you appear more human.

■ **Determine existing knowledge.** Do not waste time covering material the trainee already knows. As mentioned in Chapter 2, adults have previous knowledge or skills that should be tapped.

■ **Provide an overview.** Explain your purpose for the training along with any specific jargon, processes, or materials used during the program. This helps trainees mentally adjust and prepare for their upcoming experience.

One-on-one training.

Conducting Training

On the day of training, arrive at the site early to verify that everything is in order. If you are in a site other than the workplace, use a checklist to ensure that planned items are present and working. After your trainees arrive, check that they understand the objectives of the training as well as your role and theirs.

As the training progresses, effectively using the skills outlined in Chapter 3 becomes vital. Because of individual learning styles, you must constantly send and receive a variety of verbal and nonverbal messages while simultaneously encouraging trainees' involvement.

Assigning Tasks.   Much of the trainees' success depends on how well you plan and communicate task assignments. Whether the tasks are role-playing, performance practice sessions, or tests, let the trainees know specific information before asking them to perform. You also have to provide feedback. Here are some potential areas to consider when assigning tasks.

- **Relate instruction to the workplace.** Adults need to see real-world applications for what they learn. Taking the time to explain why and how the training will help on the job increases their commitment.

- **Define next steps.** Explain what follow-up action they must take once the task is completed. Will they have to file an after-action report? Brief others on results? Participate in additional activities? Receive feedback from you or their peers?

- **Familiarize with the task.** If you are asking your trainees to perform a new task with which they have little or no previous experience, take the time to explain and demonstrate first. Try the following steps:

  1. Explain what you want them to do.
  2. Show any equipment or materials involved and explain their purpose and function.

5

3. Demonstrate how to perform, explaining each step as you go and soliciting questions and feedback.

4. Have trainees explain the performance steps of the task while you listen, give feedback, or make corrections as necessary.

5. Have trainees perform, explaining each step, while you provide performance feedback.

6. Solicit comments about what the employee did right or could have done differently, provide constructive criticism, and praise portions done correctly.

7. If a trainee has not mastered the process, return to step 3 and repeat until the trainee successfully completes the task accurately.

By following these steps, you are including all the learning styles discussed in Chapter 2. The trainees see you perform (visual learning style), hear about the task (aural learning style), and actually perform it (kinesthetic learning style).

Providing Constructive Criticism.   Throughout all phases of the training you need to give feedback. Keep in mind that trainees who have not performed a task before may not get it completely right. When this occurs, use a systematic approach for giving constructive criticism after you have praised the portion they got right. Use this six-step process.[1]

1. Tell the person exactly what you observed. If possible, include facts or specific examples of what you mean. *Example:* "Jane, when you were connecting the main housing cover, you failed to replace the cotter key."

2. Explain the impact of their actions. Some trainees may not recognize the significance or end result of their performance or failure to meet standards. *Example:* "Jane, this could lead to severe damage to the main piston and the entire central housing unit if the cover vibrates off during operation."

---

[1] Derived from R. W. Lucas, *Coaching Skills: A Guide for Supervisors* (Burr Ridge, IL: Irwin Professional Publishing, 1994), pp. 51–52.

3. Solicit feedback. Be sincere in requesting information to uncover the reason for omission. There could be a misunderstanding of instructions, carelessness, or a poor attitude. The tips for questioning suggested in Chapters 3 and 6 may help you discover areas in which you can assist trainees toward improvement. *Example:* "Before we go any further, could you please walk me though the steps for reassembly of the main housing unit as you understand it?"

4. Show support and solicit possible solutions. Trainees need to know that you are there to assist them when needed. Even though you may have told them before, reinforce your commitment. In addition, they depend on you to provide insights and suggestions to help solve their problem or correct their performance deficit. *Example:* "What can I do that would aid in your understanding of the process or simplify the procedure for you?"

5. Get a commitment to improve behavior. Unless employees have a sincere desire to improve performance, your efforts are fruitless. You cannot, and should not, fix trainees' problems for them. Provide the tools and support they need to address the issues. *Example:* "Based on what we have discussed, I'm confident that you can master this process. Would you like to try it again?"

6. Reaffirm the trainees' worth. In this final opportunity to show support, let trainees know that even though they made mistakes, they have not failed. *Example:* "You have made a lot of progress and even though it's frustrating when you don't totally succeed at something you try, I'm sure you'll get the hang of this shortly. If I can be of assistance, please let me know."

Training Follow-up

As part of your preparation for the training, include a follow-up schedule for giving feedback on the training. The actual training is only the first step. There should be ongoing, postsession follow-up.

Coaching.   One real indicator of training effectiveness is trainees' performance on the job. Is there transfer of training from classroom to the workplace? If there is only limited or no application, you can assume that the training may not have been effective, after ruling out lack of materials, time, management support, and similar factors. Any or all of these factors could reduce or impair use of techniques learned in training. If these negative forces are inhibiting, eliminate them.

Getting feedback.   To ensure the feedback you need to appropriately coach and guide your trainees, ask a lot of questions as the training progresses. Here are some typical questions:

How does this apply . . . ?

What comes next?

Where would you use/do this?

When would it be appropriate to do/use . . . ?

Why is this valuable on the job?

Whose responsibility is it to do . . . ?

By asking these open-ended questions throughout the training process, you can determine how effective you have been explaining or demonstrating. You can also assess the trainees' understanding of what has been covered and what you need to review.

■ Expanding on What You Have Learned

With the information and techniques provided in this chapter in mind, take a few minutes to think about and respond to the following questions:

1. Opportunities to train employees one-on-one arise all the time. Can you list several that occur in your workplace?

_____

_____

2. What problems do you encounter in one-on-one training in your workplace?

_____

_____

3. How can you use the steps, processes, and information from this chapter to overcome the problems listed in question 2?

_____

_____

4. Think of an upcoming one-on-one training situation. What steps will you take to prepare for and conduct this training?

_____

_____

5

Chapter 5 Checkpoints

When planning for and conducting one-on-one training, consider the following.

- ✓ One-on-one training falls into formal and informal training categories.

- ✓ Preparation of the training and the trainees is key to ensuring success.

- ✓ When assigning tasks, taking time to explain what, why, and how trainees are performing a task is necessary to gain their commitment.

- ✓ Giving and receiving feedback helps ensure trainees' understanding and the effectiveness of the training.

- ✓ After concluding the training, there must be ongoing monitoring, follow-up and feedback.

6 | Group Presentation Skills

This chapter will help you to: ───────

- Identify the three main parts of a presentation.
- Develop techniques to focus participants' attention on you and your topic.
- Select activities that get trainees involved.
- Use questions effectively during training.

Freddie Sein, engineering supervisor at OutelSystems, was frustrated. He and his manager, Sarah Mitchell, sat in the break room discussing the first of several training programs he is delivering this month. "Sarah, I don't understand what went wrong in my session today," declared Freddie. "I read the book on presentations you gave me, and I went through the steps of the training process model. But, I still didn't get through to several of my trainees."

Sarah responded, "From what I saw, you did fine on facilitating activities and delivering your program information. You did have a little difficulty with a couple of people. Those two in the rear of the room said virtually nothing all day. And, the know-it-all up front seemed to be intentionally trying to make you look bad." She continued, "Initially, you appeared very nervous, but don't worry, everything will fall into place with more practice." ■

■ **Q u e s t i o n s   t o   C o n s i d e r**

Is the situation Freddie experienced unusual? Explain.

_____

_____

Have you ever been in a training program with the types of people described? How did you or the trainer handle them?

_____

_____

Based on this situation, how could you potentially change the program outcome?

_____

_____

EFFECTIVE OPENINGS

Whenever you step in front of a group, you become the focus of their attention. Within 30 to 90 seconds they form a positive or negative opinion of you, depending on what you say or do and how you present yourself nonverbally. For that reason, always ensure that you are totally prepared and that everything is exactly as you planned it *before* participants arrive. As you begin your presentation, review the tips in Chapters 2 and 5. To capture the interest of your audience, you can use any number of innovative openers. Limited only by your creativity and ability, these openers fall into four categories:

1. Startling statements in which you use quotes, statistics, facts, or shocking information to introduce your topic. If you were creating a program for other supervisors, you might make the following statement to both grab their attention and add a bit of humor: "I have spoken with each of your supervisors before the program. All agreed that if you do not participate actively in this session, your performance could drop and your jobs might be in jeopardy."

Even if this statement bends the truth slightly, it may not be completely false! Such a statement could potentially

- Gain attention.
- Get people involved mentally.
- Tune everyone in to you.

- Stimulate thought.
- Add humor.
- Generate a response.

2. Analogies include references to something people already know. The key is to be fairly certain that everyone in your audience has the same base knowledge about the referenced material; otherwise, the analogy is meaningless to some. As the workplace becomes more diverse, there is a wider range of backgrounds, values, and experiences. Thus, what you consider common experiences may not be common for some people. For example, a U.S.-born trainee may be thoroughly familiar with football and baseball and their associated terminology, while many foreign-born trainees may not. Therefore, if you use an analogy related to one of those sports, some people may not get the point.

Assuming you have a program with all U.S.-born participants and wanted to use an analogy to explain the importance of having established learning objectives when presenting a training session, you might use the following analogy: "Whenever I think of the result of a training program without objectives, I think of how Christopher Columbus must have felt on his voyage to America: he didn't know exactly where he was going when he started. He didn't know where he was when he got here. And when he returned home, he wasn't sure where he had been! By using such an analogy, you could

- Relate the topic to something everyone knows (Columbus).
- Help participants understand the importance of having objectives to guide trainees' learning.
- Reduce subconscious anxiety caused by a feeling that everything is going to be new.

3. Share a personal story or experience to help you relax. This often works because you are talking about something you know well—you. It also helps participants get to know you. You can relate any experience that might tie into the session topic, then open up for questions or comments, such as; "Have any of you ever experienced something similar?" "How did you handle it?" or "What happened?" By taking this approach, you

- Self-disclose.
- Demonstrate that you are human and approachable.
- Potentially bond with trainees because they can now relate based on similar experiences.
- Encourage participation, sharing, or questions.

4. Humor can release tension as well as relax you and your audience. The key is to use humor carefully and make sure whatever you use relates to the topic. Do not tell a joke simply for the sake of telling it. Additionally, if you have been told that you are not funny or if people usually do not laugh at your attempts at humor, try another type of opening. You do not want to start off trying to recover from a flop. And, if

Humor can relieve tension.

there is any possibility that any person could be offended by your humor, don't take that risk. Using humor

- Gains attention.
- Leads into your topic.
- Shows you are approachable and do not take yourself too seriously.

■ **Personal Reflection**

Think of presentations or training you have attended. What creative techniques to gain attention or lead into program topics have you seen?

_____

_____

6

SETTING THE STAGE FOR LEARNING

Once you have gotten participants' attention, explain the program objectives and solicit additional objectives from your participants. It is helpful to record their objectives on a flipchart page to post for reference at the end of the program. This reminder helps you meet all stated and defined objectives. If objectives offered by participants are not part of your program, tell them so and suggest alternate references or sessions to help them get needed information.

Adding Structure

To ensure that you cover all planned points in a logical sequence and within time limits, always use a lesson plan, outline, or notes for reference. Structure ensures the quality of your program since you stay on schedule and everyone working through your sessions gets the same information. Generally, a lesson plan for a presentation contains three sections: an introduction, body, and conclusion.

Sample Transition Phrases

To begin your transition statements, try using one of the following phrases:

After you do (have, finish) . . . you should . . .

And that brings me to . . .

Another point (step, idea, way) . . .

Another possibility is . . .

Before you . . . you should . . .

Consequently . . .

Following . . . you should . . .

In addition to . . .

Keeping in mind . . . let's examine . . .

Let's now take a look at . . .

Next . . .

Now let's talk about . . .

On the other hand . . .

The next step (phase, point) . . .

There are several ways . . . let's look at . . .

Therefore . . .

Sample Lesson Plan Cover Sheet

LESSON TITLE

Author:	I. M. Supervisor
Preparation date:	January 1, 1994
Revision date:	(Review and update yearly)
Time required:	Eight hours
Instructors required:	One primary One assistant
Training materials:	Handouts Job aids Workbooks Pencils Papers
Study assignment:	Complete post-test
Training aids or equipment:	Overhead projector Screen Transparencies Flipchart Markers (assorted colors) Masking tape
Instructor references:	(List references used to prepare content)
Learning strategies:	Self-assessment Small group discussion Video Lecture

---

6

- **Introduction.** The introduction includes one of the openers described earlier, program objectives, and a motivating statement to explain What's In It For Me (WIIFM) or what the Added Value And Results For Me (AVARFM) are to participants. Trainees who fail to recognize any personal value from being attentive to your message have little incentive to participate in your session.

- **Body.** As the meat of the program, the body includes details about the topics, time limits, activities, visual and learner aids, and questions to

Sample Lesson Outline

I. **INTRODUCTION** (30 Minutes)

    A. **Attention gainer.** Choose one of the four opening techniques outlined in this chapter.

    B. **Motivate.** Explain WIIFM and AVARFM to trainees.

    C. **Main ideas.** Define what you will cover in the session.
        1.
        2.
        3.

    D. **Objectives.** At the end of this session, trainees should be able to:
        1.
        2.
        3.

    TRANSITION: Now that you know . . .

II. **BODY**

    A. **Key idea or topic** (30 Minutes) (Handout) (Transparency)
        1. Subtopic
        2. Subtopic
           a.
           b.

    TRANSITION: Next, let's examine . . .

    B. **Key idea or topic** (25 Minutes) (Workbook) (Flipchart)
        1.
        2.

    TRANSITION: Let's review what we've covered today . . .

III. **CONCLUSION:** (10 Minutes)

    A. **Summary.** (Review of key points)

    B. **Question and answer period.**

    C. **Remotivate.** (Reinforce WIIFM/AVARFM)

ask throughout the program. In the body, you can use one or more of the activities in Chapter 4 to involve participants, facilitate learning, and discuss numerous key ideas or topics.

In presenting information, as you move from one key idea to the next, use a *transition phrase* (see samples on page 62.). These phrases are merely interjections to help you flow smoothly to your next main idea. For example, "Now that we have examined *(key idea 1),* let's move on to discuss how *(key idea 2)* can be incorporated into our system." Using such phrases prevents the uncomfortable and distracting "ahs," "ums," and "uhs" many people use to fill verbal pauses as they think of their next words. Transitions also help link ideas together.

- **Conclusion.** In the concluding section, you bring the program to a structured ending. Normally, you can paraphrase key points and make connections to the session's WIIFM/AVARFM from the introduction.

USING QUESTIONS EFFECTIVELY

Asking questions is an important skill for all supervisors and trainers. As we saw in Chapter 3, asking good questions is the hallmark of a practiced trainer. During training, questioning can help you accomplish these goals:

- Determine understanding.
- Review key points.
- Verify feelings.
- Probe for information.
- Involve participants.
- Explore opinions.
- Clarify issues.
- Raise or introduce new topics.

Various types of questions meet the preceding goals. They include the following:

- **Open-ended.** An open-ended question probes the trainees' knowledge of a topic, gets them involved, has them share their knowledge or expertise, and encourages thinking. *Example:* "Cindy, we talked earlier about effectively answering the phone. Why do you think it is important to follow the steps we outlined?"

- **Closed-end.** While valuable for verifying facts or previously identi-
fied information, a closed-end question adds little or no new information.
Often this question receives short answer or yes/no responses. *Example:*
"Jeff, did you say earlier that you have used this procedure before?"

- **Reflective or mirror.** Often used to paraphrase or reissue the question to its originator, reflective or mirror questions are good for clarifying
issues or insights and double-checking understanding. *Example:* "So, it
sounds like you think that it is important to always follow stated policy
when dealing with complaints—is that right?" or "Am I correct in believ-
ing that you think we need to stay within established guidelines?"

- **Directive.** Directive questions are good for getting new perspectives
or reviewing factual information. *Example:* "Laurie, what are the five
phases of the training process model?"

RESPONDING EFFECTIVELY

Just as important as asking the right questions is responding correctly to
questions. When someone asks you a question, follow this procedure:

- Recognize the person. "Larry, did you have a question?"

- Listen carefully to the question. Let the person finish before
responding.

- Think about what was asked. Avoid the temptation to give a standard
response because you have heard the question before or because you
have a preconceived response.

- Repeat or paraphrase the question. Paraphrasing ensures that you
interpreted the question correctly. "It sounds like your question is . . ."

- Verify the question. Verifying could save you time answering what
you thought was the question, only to have the trainee say, "That's not
really what I meant." Be sure to ask, "Was that your question, Larry?"

■ Provide a response. To encourage the involvement of others and to prevent looking like the person with all the answers, turn the question over to someone in the audience for a response before giving your own answer or opinion. "Sue, what do you think Larry could do in that situation?"

Another option is to return the question to its originator. "Interesting question, Larry. Can you think of any way to handle that situation?"

■ Verify satisfaction with the response. Do not assume you have resolved the issue. The person may even have a second question as a result of you response. Always ask, "Larry, did that answer your question?"

Do's and Don'ts for Effective Training

Do	Don't
▪ Use a checklist.	▪ Provide excessive amounts of information at one time.
▪ Plan your training activities.	
▪ Involve employees in planning and during training.	▪ Treat employees like children.
	▪ Talk down to or criticize trainees.
▪ Use other line managers or experienced employees.	▪ Use jargon or technical terms unfamiliar to trainees.
▪ Set program objectives.	▪ Ignore negative nonverbal cues from trainees.
▪ Set up an environment that aids learning.	▪ Expect everyone to progress at the same pace.
▪ Solicit information and understanding regularly.	▪ Be afraid to say, "I don't know, but I'll find out and let you know."
▪ Smile and send positive nonverbal messages.	▪ Allow a few people to dominate discussion.
▪ Ask specific, open-ended questions and wait for a response.	▪ Do all the talking.
▪ Listen carefully.	

Expanding on What You Have Learned

Facilitating group training is exciting and challenging, but takes practice to perfect. Based on information in this chapter, take a few minutes to answer these questions:

1. Do training programs at your organization contain an effective opening? If not, how could you improve these programs?

   _____

   _____

2. How are notes or outlines for programs currently formatted in your organization? What information from this chapter can you use in future program materials?

   _____

   _____

3. How can questioning techniques improve communication in your training and in daily encounters with others?

   _____

   _____

6

Chapter 6 Checkpoints

✓ Plan and prepare everything before participants arrive for training.

✓ Use an effective opening to grab the attention of trainees.

✓ Explain program objectives and solicit trainee objectives at the beginning of your programs.

✓ Add structure to your lesson plan to ensure all planned points, activities, and sequences are followed.

✓ Be conscious of the effective ideas listed in this chapter when planning a program.

✓ When questioning, use an assortment of question types to clarify, verify, involve, and probe.

7 | Using Training Aids

This chapter will help you to: ────────────

- Select appropriate training aids.
- Recognize the importance of training aids in reinforcing learning.
- Use training aids effectively.

Roger Walker's first day of training deteriorated rapidly. Due to severe traffic congestion, he arrived only 20 minutes before the class was to begin. The overhead projector bulb blew and it took Roger five minutes to change it. His handouts were stapled in the wrong order. Throughout the day, he was plagued with missing, broken, or inappropriate equipment and material. Needless to say, by the end of the day Roger was a wreck. Trainees' evaluations revealed that most trainees thought the experience was a waste of time. ■

■ Questions to Consider

What could Roger have done to prevent this disaster?

_____

_____

Do you believe that others share blame for any of the mishaps in this scenario? Explain.

_____

_____

Why are planning and follow through so important in a training program?

_____

_____

PLANNING

You can avoid duplicating Roger's problems by thinking ahead, planning, and following through before trainees arrive. To help accomplish this, prepare a checklist such as the one in this chapter and add or delete items as necessary. Also, you need to effectively identify and learn to use training aids.

Common Training Aids

- Overhead projector.
- VCR and monitor.
- 35mm slide projector.
- Flipchart pad and easel.
- Dry erase board.
- Audiotape player.
- Charts.

To be valuable resources, you must properly use any training aids you choose for your programs. We'll examine specific types later in this chapter along with tips for their effective use. While each training aid has different strengths and weaknesses as a teaching tool, here are some tips for using all types:

- **Think before choosing.** Ask yourself the following questions before deciding on a specific type of training aid. When the answer to any question is *no*, look for an alternative. Is the training aid

  - Going to complement the spoken message?
  - Necessary?
  - Relevant to course content?
  - Economical?
  - Available?
  - Easy to use?
  - Durable (can you reuse it)?
  - Easy to understand?

- **Supplement your spoken message.** The biggest mistake many supervisors make in using training aids is trying to let the aid teach. Training aids should enhance and clarify your spoken message; they cannot replace you as an instructor. An example of improper usage would be showing a video that you have not previewed or introduced to trainees, leaving the room, returning when the video ends, then moving on with the program without debriefing key points in the video. In this instance, there could have been inappropriate or confusing information in the video, or the video could have malfunctioned, leaving your trainees sitting in the dark.

- **Ensure that everyone can see and hear.** Before trainees arrive, play the audiovisual aid and move to the farthest points in the room to ensure the aid's visibility and audibility from any location.

- **Have accessories available.** Using a checklist, ensure that all necessary additional or replacement items are on hand to prepare for all contingencies.

7

- **Familiarize yourself with usage.** Practice your presentation, including the use of your training aids, until you are thoroughly familiar and comfortable with the way the program information flows. Various manufacturers design their equipment differently. Do not assume that all projectors or other types of equipment work the same.

- **Be flexible.** Even though your lesson plan calls for a transparency, be willing to skip it or use a different training aid. For example, you may have planned to use a transparency illustrating a process, but because of a trainee's question you use a flipchart of key points instead. Later, when you arrive at the scheduled point to discuss the process, you would show the original transparency to reiterate and reinforce your information.

Personal Reflection

Think about a training program where things obviously did not go well, because the instructor seemed unprepared, equipment was missing or broken, materials were out of sequence or ineffective.

What did you think of the instructor?

_____

_____

How did you feel throughout the day? At the end of the program?

_____

_____

KNOW YOUR EQUIPMENT

A training aid is anything that you can use in a session to clarify ideas, concepts, or information, or to reinforce learning. To appeal to various learning styles, use a variety of training aids in your program. We discuss some of the more common aids starting on page 76.

TRAINING CHECKLIST

Program _____

Date _____

Training Aids/Materials

_____ Leader's guide.

_____ Participant workbook.

_____ Handouts.

_____ Videos.

_____ Transparencies.

Overhead Projector

_____ Spare bulb (test bulb in projector).

_____ Cleaned of lint and fingerprints.

VCR/Monitor

_____ Placed for best viewing by all.

_____ On correct channel.

_____ Videos cued to beginning.

_____ Tracking adjusted on videos.

_____ Volume on monitor adjusted.

_____ Remote control (with batteries).

Music

_____ Tapes cued.

_____ Volume adjusted.

Screen

_____ Location/adjusted to 90-degree angle to prevent keystoning (distorted projected image where the top is wider than the bottom).

_____ Appropriate size.

Flipchart

_____ Paper in place.

_____ Predesigned flipcharts drawn.

_____ Markers (assorted colors).

_____ Pages tabbed.

_____ Flipcharts and easels in place.

_____ Masking tape.

_____ Focused and positioned.

_____ First transparency in place.

_____ Radio on channel.

7

Actual Items

Actual items the trainees will use on the job are always the best aids. They provide practical, realistic, job-related practice and exposure. For example, if you are training people in using a word processing software system, use the exact version they will use on the job to reduce confusion and frustration later.

Basic Tips

- Provide one item for each trainee, if possible.
- Ensure that the item is functioning properly and is the same model the trainee will use on the job.
- Cover any necessary safety guidelines if the trainee has never used the item before. Also, provide enough room to use the device so no one gets injured.

Charts

Charts are effective for graphically displaying statistics, trends, information flow, and other sequential data.

Basic Tips

- Ensure that you understand all information on the chart and can accurately explain it to others.
- Position the chart so that everyone can view it easily.
- Include up to three colors to increase interest and effectiveness. If more colors are needed, use shades of the three chosen colors.
- Ensure accuracy of information and spelling.
- Display the chart only when you are ready to discuss it, then put it away.

Dry Erase or Chalkboards

After the initial purchase, dry erase or chalkboards are an inexpensive means of providing impromptu or prewritten information. Just as with flipcharts, check the board's visibility at various distances. Also, be aware of good usage techniques, your positioning as you write, color and size of lettering, and neatness of writing.

Basic Tips

- Ensure you have a variety of colored markers or chalk specially created to write on the intended surface. Black, blue, green, and brown are good for visibility. Red can be used for key words.
- Have an eraser available.
- Do not talk when writing. Finish writing, then face your audience to speak.

Flipcharts

Flipcharts can be predesigned or used spontaneously during training to capture ideas or clarify key points. With lettering 1½ to 2 inches in height, you can use them up to 25 feet from your audience.

Basic Tips

- Make sure the easel legs are locked into position and balanced for ease of writing.
- Use no-bleed, water-based markers to prevent ink from seeping through to the next page.
- Leave a blank sheet of paper between prewritten pages to prevent trainees from reading the next page or in case markers bleed.
- Use six to eight lines per page and avoid using the bottom one-third of the page to ensure visibility from the rear of the room.

- Place only one topic or idea per page.
- Do not talk to the flipchart while writing.
- Put the marker down when not writing to prevent distractions.
- Use no more than three vertical columns of data per page.

Transparencies

You can produce transparencies relatively easily using a variety of computer software programs, printers, and plain paper copiers. They are versatile and can produce colors, graphics, and text to enhance your message. Additionally, transparencies are durable and travel well when you have to move your training to various remote locations.

Basic Tips

- Ensure the projector is focused and the transparency is straight on the projection surface.
- Do not stand between the screen and participants.
- Turn the projector off or cover the projection surface when not addressing the points on a transparency.
- Use upper-case lettering for title lines and upper/lower case for text. Avoid using strictly upper case because it is difficult to read.
- Never use typewriter size (10 point) lettering. Letters should be at least one-quarter inch high. An easy gauge is to create your transparency, place it on the floor, and stand straight above it. If you can read it clearly, it is probably visible up to 25 or 30 feet from the screen.
- Follow a standard format, either printed vertically (8½ × 11) or horizontally (11 × 8½) on the film. Changing formats is distracting.
- Include topic-related graphics, if possible.
- Limit text to 8 to 10 lines and words to six to eight per line.

Videos

Videos are excellent aids when training on virtually any workplace topic or skills set. You can purchase off-the-shelf versions or produce your own in-house. If you need a specialized focus, you can also contract with a video production company to customize a topic to fit your organization's training need.

Basic Tips
- Use to enhance your program, not replace yourself.
- Ensure equipment works before trainees arrive.
- Cue tapes to the beginning before trainees arrive.
- Rewind tapes after use to prepare for next usage.
- Make sure video content is appropriate for the program and audience, and information is current.

Audiocassettes

Audiocassettes allow trainees to hear specific examples of a technique you have explained. For example, if you were doing a course on verbal communication and wanted to demonstrate the voice qualities of intonation, rate of speech, inflection, or volume, audiocassettes would be an ideal medium. As with videos, audiocassettes come prerecorded or can be made inexpensively.

Basic Tips
- Ensure the equipment works before trainees arrive.
- Cue tapes to the beginning before trainees arrive.
- Check the volume before the program begins.

35mm Slides

Slides are good aids due to their quality and size. However, they have serious limitations and work better in shorter presentations. To use slides effectively, you must darken the room, have a large screen to view them, and position yourself where you can operate the projector without obscuring any trainee's view. Also, you must position yourself where you can read from the screen.

Basic Tips

- Use sparingly.
- Use remote control, if available.
- Place projector where the projected image is not blocked by someone's head.
- Check to see that the slides are in proper sequence and not upside down before trainees arrive.
- Have a spare bulb and carousel available.

Effective use of training aids enhances your verbal message.

■ Expanding on What You Have Learned

Using training aids effectively can add to the value of your presentation.

1. What training aids are currently being used in your organization's training program?

   _____

   _____

2. How could training programs be improved with new or different training aids?

   _____

   _____

3. What resources are available to assist you in designing, developing, or obtaining training aids and equipment for your training programs?

   _____

   _____

4. How can you tie information from this chapter into that of the previous ones to improve your training effectiveness?

   _____

   _____

7

Chapter 7 Checkpoints

When designing or preparing a future training program consider the following:

✓ Use checklists to ensure that you have all necessary material, equipment, and training aids before participants arrive.

✓ Training aids consist of anything that clarifies and reinforces training ideas, concepts, and information.

✓ Actual items are best as training aids because they give realistic, job-related practice or exposure.

✓ Use a variety of training aids for maximum learning reinforcement.

8 | Professional Development

This chapter will help you to:

- Identify resources to enhance training.
- Find organizations for training partnerships.
- Tap into resources to develop your training knowledge and skills.

Leslie Kirchner has just confided in fellow supervisor, Annette Madeline, that she wants to project a more confident and knowledgeable image concerning training. During the conversation, Leslie declared, "I know a lot of organizations and vendors must deal with organizational training issues, but I don't know how to find them."

Annette could relate to Leslie's frustration. As a new supervisor several years ago, she had similar concerns. Annette told Leslie about a listing of resources she had developed that she would be happy to share. She suggested that Leslie start her own information search by going to see the reference librarian at the public library. Leslie responded, "These are great ideas, Annette. I'll get started today. As soon as I get your list, I'll contact those sources, too. Thanks." ∎

▌ Questions to Consider

Have you ever felt that you needed information or assistance with a workplace task but did not know where to seek help? Where did you start?

_____

_____

What else could Annette have done to assist Leslie?

_____

_____

TRAINING RESOURCES

In thinking about this scenario and answering the questions, you have begun to develop your own training resource listing. There is no great secret to identifying individuals or organizations to help with your training needs. The best starting place is often your current network of peers, vendors, employees, friends, and business contacts.

Local Resources

On the local level, you can often get information, ideas, and funding by making a few phone calls or by networking in the business community.

- **Partnerships.** A new trend in today's competitive business environment is to merge resources with other organizations. Other local businesses or government agencies that have training programs provide products and services similar to your organization's and are wrestling with needs and issues similar to yours. By contacting the training or human resources departments of those organizations, you may find someone willing to share or exchange training programs, materials, or resources. This partnering can save time, effort, and money.

- **Networking.** Many chambers of commerce, businesses, professional associations, vendors, and higher education facilities have social functions throughout the year (luncheons, after-hours receptions, silent auctions, or fund raisers). These provide perfect opportunities to meet people and expand your network. For tips on how to effectively meet and network, you may want to review ideas in another book in this series, *Effective Interpersonal Relationships.*

- **Vendors.** Organizations that provide training supplies, equipment, videos, services, and programs are often happy to come to your location for consultation or to display their wares. Often, you can get low-cost items or free video previews and garner additional contacts while meeting with their representatives. Even if you do not buy from all of the organizations you contact, you can develop a keen awareness of what is on the market and fair value costs, in the event you need to seriously shop in the future. You can also develop a resource listing for future reference.

- **Professional publications.** Many of the organizations listed later in this chapter publish books, magazines, and vendor listings as a service to their members. Even if you do not join the group, you can often subscribe to its publication, borrow it from a colleague, or get it through the library.

- **Research services.** On-line computer searches for articles, organizations, and information are available through most public, college, and university libraries. Similarly, you can obtain additional information through professional organizations. The U.S. Library of Congress and the Government Printing Office in Washington, D.C., are also valuable sources of information.

- **State grants.** In many states, funding is available through state agencies or colleges to organizations that relocate or hire significant numbers of employees. These funds are available to help organizations to expand or develop new products and services. The money is often designated for training programs and equipment.

- **Professional development programs.** Various organizations offer professional development programs throughout the United States in many major cities at an economical cost. By contacting the organizations listed in this chapter, attending their conferences, or reading training management publications, you can identify sources for these programs. Once you make contact, request to be added to their mailing lists for future program announcements. Many of these program vendors can give programs tailored to your training needs at your location. This reduces program costs and related travel expenses, while providing training to a wider number of employees.

■ **Continuing education courses.** Most major colleges and universities now offer business programs and degrees that include human resource and training development courses. Often, you can partner with the institution to conduct the classes at your organizational training facility. Another option would be to partner with a neighboring organization with needs similar to yours.

National Resources

With the government's concerted interest and emphasis on training, as well as the increase in private training organizations and individuals, finding information and resources nationwide is getting easier. Numerous publications contain detailed listings of phone numbers and contact people. Here are some prominent sources in the United States. Many also have local offices or chapters listed in your local telephone directory.

- American Management Association
  AMACON Division
  135 West 50th Street
  New York, NY 10020
  (212) 586-8100

- American Society for Quality Control
  310 West Wisconsin Avenue
  Milwaukee, WI 53203
  (414) 272-8575

- American Society for Training & Development
  PO Box 1443
  1640 King Street
  Alexandria, VA 22313-9833
  (703) 683-8100

- Association for Sales Training
  PO Box 2902
  Palos Verdes, CA 90274
  (213) 378-2666

- International Personnel Management Association
  1617 Duke Street
  Alexandria, VA 22314
  (703) 549-7100

- National Society for Performance & Instruction
  1300 L Street NW, Suite 1250
  Washington, DC 20005
  (202) 408-7969

- Professional Organizational Development Network
  c/o David Graf
  Instructional Development Office
  Exhibit Hall South
  Iowa State University
  Ames, IA 50011
  (515) 294-2316

- Training Directors Forum
  50 South Ninth Street
  Minneapolis, MN 55402
  (612) 333-0471, Ext 508

8

■ Expanding on What You Have Learned

Tapping into available resources can save you quite a bit of time and trouble.

1. In addition to suggestions in this chapter, which organizations in your local area can provide listings or potential training resources?

   _____

   _____

2. Whom do you know, inside or outside your organization, who can provide training and might be a potential partner?

   _____

   _____

Chapter 8 Checkpoints

✓ Begin your search for information, ideas, and resources at the local level, using suggestions from this chapter.

✓ Work at developing partnerships, networking, and using a variety of resources to save time, effort, and money.

✓ Look to state and national organizations and agencies to expand your resource bank.

Post-Test

Take a few minutes to test your understanding of the key concepts in *Training Skills for Supervisors*. Once you have completed the test, check your answers and review any areas where you had difficulty.

True   **False**

_____   _____   **1.** Training is a good intervention whenever an employee experiences performance problems.

_____   _____   **2.** Adults learn new information in basically the same manner as children.

_____   _____   **3.** You can sometimes determine people's learning style preferences by the way they phrase sentences or ask questions.

_____   _____   **4.** Supervisors often make good trainers.

_____   _____   **5.** You should identify training needs before developing or providing employee training.

_____   _____   **6.** Feedback is a key component in all phases of the training process model.

_____   _____   **7.** Because of the expense involved, real, job-related items should only be used in training as a last resort.

_____   _____   **8.** It is important to use a checklist whenever you conduct training.

_____   _____   **9.** One-on-one training falls into only the formal category.

_____   _____   **10.** Virtually hundreds of resources are available at the local and national level to assist you in your training efforts.

ANSWER KEY

1. *False.*   2. *False.*   3. *True.*   4. *True.*   5. *True.*   6. *True.*

7. *False.*   8. *True.*   9. *False.*   10. *True.*

Business Skills Express Series

This growing series of books addresses a broad range of key business skills and topics to meet the needs of employees, human resource departments, and training consultants.

To obtain information about these and other Business Skills Express books, please call IRWIN Professional Publishing toll free at: 1-800-634-3966.

Effective Performance Management
ISBN   1-55623-867-3

Hiring the Best
ISBN   1-55623-865-7

Writing that Works
ISBN   1-55623-856-8

Customer Service Excellence
ISBN   1-55623-969-6

Writing for Business Results
ISBN   1-55623-854-1

Powerful Presentation Skills
ISBN   1-55623-870-3

Meetings that Work
ISBN   1-55623-866-5

Effective Teamwork
ISBN   1-55623-880-0

Time Management
ISBN   1-55623-888-6

Assertiveness Skills
ISBN   1-55623-857-6

Motivation at Work
ISBN   1-55623-868-1

Overcoming Anxiety at Work
ISBN   1-55623-869-X

Positive Politics at Work
ISBN   1-55623-879-7

Telephone Skills at Work
ISBN   1-55623-858-4

Managing Conflict at Work
ISBN   1-55623-890-8

The New Supervisor: Skills for Success
ISBN   1-55623-762-6

The *Americans with Disabilities Act*: What Supervisors Need to Know
ISBN   1-55623-889-4

Managing the Demands of Work and Home
ISBN   0-7863-0221-6

Effective Listening Skills
ISBN   0-7863-0102-4

Goal Management at Work
ISBN   0-7863-0225-9

Positive Attitudes at Work
ISBN   0-7863-0100-8

Supervising the Difficult Employee
ISBN   0-7863-0219-4

Cultural Diversity in the Workplace
ISBN   0-7863-0125-2

Managing Change in the Workplace
ISBN   0-7863-0162-7

Negotiating for Business Results
ISBN   0-7863-0114-7

Practical Business Communication
ISBN   0-7863-0227-5

High Performance Speaking
ISBN   0-7863-0222-4

Delegation Skills
ISBN   0-7863-0105-9

Coaching Skills: A Guide for Supervisors
ISBN   0-7863-0220-8

Customer Service and the Telephone
ISBN   0-7863-0224-0

Creativity at Work
ISBN   0-7863-0223-2

Effective Interpersonal Relationships
ISBN   0-7863-0255-0

The Participative Leader
ISBN   0-7863-0252-6

Building Customer Loyalty
ISBN   0-7863-0253-4

Getting and Staying Organized
ISBN   0-7863-0254-2

Total Quality Selling
ISBN   0-7863-0324-7

Business Etiquette
ISBN   0-7863-0323-9

Empowering Employees
ISBN   0-7863-0314-X

Training Skills for Supervisors
ISBN   0-7863-0313-1

Moving Meetings
ISBN   0-7863-0333-6

Multicultural Customer Service
ISBN   0-7863-0332-8